The Lost Craft
失落的技艺

Hai An

海岸

Translated by Ouyang Yu

译者：欧阳昱

PUNCHER & WATTMANN

First published in 2020
Published by Puncher and Wattmann
PO Box 279
Waratah NSW 2298

http://www.puncherandwattmann.com
puncherandwattmann@bigpond.com

NATIONAL
LIBRARY
OF AUSTRALIA

A catalogue entry for this book is available from the National Library of Australia.

ISBN   9781925780802

Printed by Lightning Source International

Contents

【作者简介】

海岸，诗人、翻译家，原名李定军，浙江台州人，1980年代毕业于杭州大学外语系、上海医科大学研究生院，现为复旦大学《英汉医学大词典》主编，复旦中澳创意写作中心／复旦文学翻译研究中心学者，先后获得过国家社会科学基金、首届上海高校服务国家重大战略出版工程基金、上海文化发展基金、上海翻译家协会"STA翻译成就奖"等。著有《海岸诗选》（2001）、《海岸短诗选》（2003，香港）、《挽歌》（长诗，2012，台湾）、《蝴蝶·蜻蜓》（欧洲 Point Editions 2019）、《时光，像一座奔跑的坟墓——狄兰·托马斯诗歌翻译与批评》（2020），译有《狄兰·托马斯诗选》（2002/2014/2015）、《贝克特全集：诗集》（合译，2016）、《流水光阴——杰曼·卓根布鲁特诗选》（荷兰，2019），编有《中西诗歌翻译百年论集》（2007）、《中国当代诗歌前浪》（欧洲／青海，汉英对照，2009）、《归巢与启程：中澳当代诗选》（合编，汉英对照，2018）等。曾应邀参加"第15届阿根廷罗萨里奥国际诗歌节"（2007）、"第48届马其顿斯特鲁加国际诗歌之夜"（2009）、"罗马尼亚米哈伊·艾米内斯库国际诗歌节"（2014）、"复旦－科廷中澳创意写作坊"（2016-2019）等海内外诗歌活动。

Biographical Note

Born in 1965 in Taizhou, Zhejiang, Hai An, Chinese scholar-poet and translator, whose real name is LI Dingjun, was the winner of Chinese National Social Sciences Fund, Shanghai Universities and Colleges Major Strategic Publishing Project Fund for National Service, Shanghai Cultural Development Fund, and STA Translation Achievements Award issued by Shanghai Translator Association. He graduated from the Department of Foreign Languages, Hangzhou University, and the Graduate School, Shanghai Medical University in the 1980s, and is now serving as editor-in-chief of *English-Chinese Medical Dictionary*, Associate Professor at College of Foreign Languages and Literatures, as well as a research scholar of Literary Translation Research Center / China-Australia Creative Writing Center, Fudan University. He has published more than ten books of poetry as the author, translator and editor, such as *Selected Poems by Hai An* (2001), *Selected Short Poems by Hai An* (Hong Kong, 2003), *Elegy: Hai An's First Therapeutic Long Poem* (2012, Taiwan), *A Butterfly & A Dragonfly* (Point Editions, Europe, 2019), *When, Like a Running Grave: A Critical Approach to Dylan Thomas's Poetry and Its Translation* (2020); *Selected Poems of Dylan Thomas* (2002, 2014, 2015), *Collected Poems of Samuel Beckett (co-translated, 2016), In the Stream of Time: Selected Poems of Germain Droogenbroodt (Holland, 2019)*; *A Centennial Collected Papers on Sino-Occidental Poetry Translation* (2007), *The Frontier Tide: Contemporary Chinese Poetry* (Europe / Qinghai, 2009), *Homings and Departure: Selected Poems from Contemporary China and Australia* (co-edited, 2018). He attended several international poetry festivals, including the 15th International Poetry Festival in Rosario, Argentina (2007), the 48th International Poetry Evening in Struga, Macedonia (2009), the International Poetry Festival of Mihai Eminescu in Craiova, Romania (2014) and China-Australia Creative Writing Workshops at Fudan and Curtin University (2016-2019).

踏青

从黄龙洞上山，攀援保俶塔下的初阳台
西湖晨露未褪
翻越葛岭，悠然进入宋词
一步三回头
牵手同窗好友，步入谷底
春花秋月，更兼残雪
大学的光阴似水

从白堤上船，驶向湖心三潭印月
挨个扶塔留影，抑或
横一叶小舟
赏苏堤六桥烟柳
听曲院风荷南屏晚钟
余音袅袅
飞越云栖九溪十八涧

午夜的影院散了场
我随《第三次浪潮》涌出湖心

（1984，西子湖畔）

Treading the Green in Spring

Climbing the mountain from the Yellow Dragon Cave, onto the Chuyangtai
Pavilion under the Baochu Pagoda
I found that the morning dew had not yet receded from the West Lake
Then I went over the Geling Ridge and, in a leisurely pace, entered into a *ci*
of Song dynasty
One step forward and three headturns
I, hand in hand with a good friend, stepped into the bottom of the valley
Where, with the spring flowers and the autumn moon, and the remaining
snow
University days had gone, like water

We took a boat from the White Dyke and sailed to the Three Pools
Mirroring the Moon in the middle of the lake
Taking turns having photos taken, leaning against the pagoda, or
We sat in the leaf of a boat
Enjoying the six-bridge smoky willows on the Su Dyke
And listening to the lingering sound
Of the Nanping evening bells amidst the lotus flowers in the breezy winding
courtyard
That flew over the nine creeks and eighteen brooks in Yunqi

As the cinema was closing at midnight
I surged out of the heart of the lake with *The Third Wave*

(1984, at the West Lake, Hangzhou)

夜之断想

夜风撩拨窗帷
淡蓝的修竹倾斜。竹花撒满一席

一个身影缓缓地垂落
一种惶惑的风姿
在清凉的石阶上随风飘荡

子夜的灯火
一舌展翅的触须
期待奔逸的雨花飘落

忧郁的表情
一树青涩的果浆
从眉梢优美地滑落

夜是一片黑色的海洋
一丝甜蜜映着天地
点点星光涂抹白色的院墙

孤岛无语。夜风吹过海门
淹没在水中自有其存在的意义

（1985，台州湾）

Fragmentary Thoughts, at Night

The night wind was stirring the curtains
As the pale-blue bamboos were leaning, their flowers spreading over the mat

A shadow, slowly, fell
With a puzzled gesture
Drifting with the wind across the cool stone steps

Lights at midnight
Tentacles on the wing of a tongue
In anticipation of the falling flowers of a rushing rain

Sad facial features
And a tree of green, astringent fruit pulp
That slipped, beautifully, off the tip of the brow

The night was an ocean of blackness
A thread of honeyed sweetness reflecting the sky and the earth
Dots of starlight smearing the white walls of the courtyard

The island, solitary and wordless. The night wind blew across sea gate
When the drowning in the water had, after all, its own significance

(1985, at the Taizhou Bay)

静静远离，片言只语仅仅远离片刻

城市相挽着，哪怕是断壁残垣
瘦削如风的肩膀没有风度
我从人流中走过
从单元音双元音铺就的轨道走过
片　言　只　语
摔下几个片断、几个情节或故事
土地和阳光从此步入背景

一次远离自己的散步
一场片言只语的对话
在某一碧野此起彼伏
或是一种简单的手势　之后
城市回归宁静
我回归一个蹲坐或蜷缩的姿态
片言只语起身离去，静静远离

顷刻。角色退出音乐之外
灯光折叠起来
我坐着，试图坐在主角的位子
干瘪的袖口盛满风
鼓动身子，一阵又一阵
追赶静静远离的言语

世界蜕换着季节的外衣
天空飘浮阳光的影子
片言只语，波动源初的水声
从破碎的岁月里
落
下

来
落在金属般龟裂的舌面
溅起一片血珠的光亮

走在城市的人流中
走在单元音双元音铺就的轨道上
我抚着旗帜般招展的城墙
片 言 只 语
在躯壳内生起
静静远离，片言只语仅仅远离片刻

(1987)

Quietly Leaving, and, Only for a Brief Moment, in Fragmentary Words

Cities, arm in arm, regardless of the debris of the broken walls

And the shoulders, thin as wind, had nothing of the wind's elegance

I was walking through the flow of the people

On the rails of monophthongs and diphthongs

Frag   men   tary   wo   rds

Throwing down fragments, plots or stories

The earth and the sun having stepped into the background from then on

A walk that moved away from itself

A dialogue that consisted of fragmentary words

Rising and fall, on a certain green plain

Or, after   a simple gesture

The city returned to stillness

As I returned to a squatting or curling posture

And the fragmentary words rose up, to leave quietly

In an instant. Characters went outside the music

Lights folded themselves

Heaving in a certain blue field

I was sitting, trying to sit in the protagonist's seat

My wizened sleeves filled with wind

Agitating my body, again and again

Giving a chase to the language moving further away in quietness

The world was changing its garments of season

And the shadows of sunlight were floating in the sky

Fragmentary words, wavy with the sound of water from the beginnings

16

Falling

From

The broken years

Onto the lie of the tongue, cracking like metal

And splashing with a spread of bloody-pearly light

Walking through the flow of the people

And on the rails of monophthongs and diphthongs

I touched the city wall, exhibited like a flag

Frag   men   tary   wo   rds

Rose from within the shell

Quietly leaving

Quietly leaving, and, only for a brief moment, in fragmentary words

(1987)

表情一二

风起了，起自某一个角落
手向内屈伸
也许不敢就位
臀下没有可坐的椅子

独自站在各种表情前
墙是身后唯一竖立的背景
恰如一个人的脸面
反弹旁人的目光若隐若现

我徘徊在空气中
没有灯火没有话语
摆动摆动空荡荡的臂膀
一对太阳穴跳动起心的存在

此时，门从一侧打开
亮光击中表情
半张脸面陷入阴影
白昼消失，也许从未存在

无奈地抬一抬手
活动一次手指去修饰脸面
胡子全已刮落
明天的表情十分简洁

(1988)

18

Expressions, One or Two

The wind rose, from a corner
And the hand bent inwards
Perhaps afraid to be seated
As there was no chair to sit beneath the buttocks

Standing alone before a variety of expressions
The wall being the only background erected behind one
Like the face of someone
Rebounding someone else's look that was half visible

I paced, to and fro, in the air
No lights, no words
Swinging, swinging, with empty arms
A pair of temples jumped into the existence of a heart

Just then, the door opened on the side
As the light hit the expression
And the half-face sank into the shadow
The day disappearing or perhaps having never existed

Helplessly, the hand raised itself
And the fingers were exercised to modify the face
When the beard was all removed
The expression for tomorrow was clean and simple

(1988)

十月的金秋已尽

午门的钟鼓远去。深秋枯黄
如意们又干又凉
宫女们的歌声远去

皇帝走过庭院，走过甬道
走下祖辈相连的台阶
他无奈地脱下皇冠
　　回望身后的过去
天冷冷地回望大地

戴皇冠与不戴皇冠的男人或女人
相继走过城楼
由远而近　由近及远
风尘抹去遗留的脚印
十月的金秋已尽

假如永远是秋天，永远是秋高气爽
叹息声传遍皇宫

(1988)

The Ending of a Golden Autumn in October

The drum and the bells at the Meridian Gate sounded distant. A deep
autumn, of withered yellow
The sceptres were dry and cool
And the singing of the imperial concubines sounded far

The emperor walked through the courtyard, down the corridor
Down the steps connected with his ancestors
Helplessly, he disrobed
    and turned to look at the past behind him
The sky, coldly, looked back down at the land

Men or women, wearing the crowns or no crowns
Successively went past the city gate tower
Getting closer   getting further
The remaining footsteps erased by the wind and dust
As the golden autumn ended in October

'If only the autumn remained eternal, always high and crisp'
The sigh was spreading through the imperial palace

(1988)

冬天坐在我的对面

伸出手推一推季节
冬天就会从半空落下
表情很冷很冷
我情不自禁地打开嘴唇
烘烘她的手指，温暖
她的距离，她的心
温暖她那双冰封的注视
然后，随随便便地扯开自己
想象一次言语的过程
从冬天进入春天
静心修饰某段曝光的日子
某张几度曝光的表情
直至夕阳西下　冰雪消融
在冬天降临的日子里
寒意适宜人们扯开想象的另一面
想象季节的背后阳光的背后
熟悉或陌生脸面的背后
想象自己
随随便便地伸出手
冬天随之落在对面的位子上

(1988)

The Winter Sitting Opposite Me

If you give a push to the season
Winter will drop out of the sky
With a cold expression
I couldn't help but open my lips
To warm her fingers, to warm
Her distance, her heart
And to warm her ice-bound stare
Before I, casually, tore myself off
To imagine a process of language
Entering into spring from winter
And composedly modifying a section of exposed days
And a number of exposed expressions
Till the sun set   the snow and ice melted
On the day the winter fell
The coldness was fitting for people to tear open the other side of
                                                    imagination
To imagine the back of the sun behind the season
Behind the faces, familiar or strange
And to imagine oneself
To casually hold out one's hand
Along with that, the winter fell on the opposite seat

(1988)

杯水之间

随手伸出一对灵活的手指
超越端坐的桌面
操起一杯水
掌心温暖，手中的水
开始颤动
手外的水面漂满了伤感

随手伸出所有活着的手指
超越肃立的墙壁
操起相对的两杯水
掌心热烈，指间的水沸腾
指外的嘴看着左右
面色渐趋苍老

随手伸出一种优美的姿势
超越南方与北方
溅湿的手指收回来
掌心宁静，杯内杯外是水
指间不见漂浮的伤感
没有忧伤没有

杯水之间搁着一双手
掌心冰凉

(1989)

Between the Glass and the Water

A pair of agile fingers that were extended, just like that
Beyond the dwelling tabletop
To pick up a glass of water
The warm heart of the hand, the water in the hand
Began shivering
The water outside the hand filled with sadness

All living fingers that were extended, just like that
Beyond the silently standing wall
To hold two glasses of water opposite each other
The passionate heart of the hand, the water boiling between the fingers
The mouth outside the fingers looked left and right
The colours of the face gradually ageing

A beautiful gesture that was extended, just like that
Beyond the north and the south
The wet fingers retrieving themselves
The still heart of the hand, water inside and outside the glass
The sadness floating between the fingers not seen
No sadness, no

A pair of hands between the glass and the water
The heart of the hand icy-cold

(1989)

雨

回望某个人的站立
流水匆匆
血液踏破皮革
轰鸣远去　满载季节的车远去

海鱼吐出最后的预言
离岸远去

那条通晓人语的鱼
那群知晓多种语言的人
一无遮掩　一无武器
头顶青天烈日
深陷水域

一场雨淋湿半个世纪
一场雨淹没地球半张脸面

(1989)

Rain

When I looked back at someone standing
I saw the flowing water in a hurry
The blood tearing the leather
Going away with a boom   a truck going away filled with seasons

The sea fish spat out the last prophecy
Going away from the bank

The fish with a knowledge of the human language
The group of people with a knowledge of many languages
No concealment   no weapons
Their heads bearing the scorching sun in the sky
Sinking deeply in the waters

A rain has drenched half a century
A rain has drowned half the face of the globe

(1989)

镜片

在距离与空气之间
唯一明亮的中心
是镜片　一副冷色的眼
在阳光与回响之间
一种波动的影子
是脸　行色匆匆的脸
我的肉眼躲在后面
两张呼喊的嘴
面对现实　梦更远
要与人对话
与镜片　我是镜片　是对手
说出的语言更添恐怖
我是人还是镜片　无人评判
置身距离的镜片微笑

(1989)

The Lens

Between distance and air

The only bright centre

Is the lens   a set of cold-coloured eyes

Between sunshine and echoes

A wavy shadow

Was the face   a hurrying face

My own naked eyes were hiding behind

Two yelling mouths

In the face of realities   dreams were further away

Must have a dialogue with people

With the lens   I'm the lens   I'm the rival

The language, when spoken, was even more terrifying

Am I a person or a lens?   No one was there to judge

Situated in the distance, the lens was smiling

(1989)

钟表是结局

钟表是结局。此刻无奈
还有垂落的手势
红润死在憔悴的言词之下
春天收购泪水
笑脸印成定量的面额
塞满所有流血的口袋
最好贴肉
此刻我们多想触及
海　心的呼吸
触及海崖上空太阳的暴怒
而钟表是结局
雪，仅有的回报
从手腕中飘落
它说要填补思想的切口

(1989)

The Clock Was the End

The clock was the end. This moment helpless

And the falling gesture

Rosiness died under the withered words

The spring was purchasing tears

When smiling faces were printed in quantitative denomination

Stuffing all the bleeding pockets

Best if they were close to the flesh

Right at this moment we'd so much like to touch

The sea   the breathing of the heart

To touch the fury of the sun above the sea cliffs

But the clock was the end

The snow, the only return

Fell drifting down the wrist

Saying that it wanted to fill the cut of thought

(1989)

我们受困。而且

无奈将自己关入躯壳。眼睛终究
抵达不了彼岸
阳光扑不灭门内的漆黑
任仅存的一对手脚寄存在人世

唯恐感染门外的世界
肉身孕育成一座避难所
拿起笔　隔着白纸
囚居自己
从此远离世界
一个躯壳远离另一个

面对喧嚣的世界
面对掌心柔软的冲动
我们沉默不语
一旦进入，自我从此消失

终将要被世界吞吃　活生生地
我们无法脱身

(1989)

We Got stuck. And

Helplessly, I got myself shut in a shell. The eye, after all, wasn't able
to reach the other shore
the sunshine could not quench the darkness inside the door
depositing the only remaining pair of hands and feet in the world

the only fear being that the world outside the door got infected
and that the body was breeding into a refuge
so, take up a pen   and prison yourself
on the other side of the paper
thus keeping far away from the world
a shell far away from another

in the face of a noisy world
and of a soft impulse in the heart of the hand
we remained silent
as soon as entry is made, the self disappears

to be swallowed alive by the world
we couldn't possibly rid ourselves of it all

(1989)

Hello, 90

我未触及彼岸，却触及
一个年代的底部。像触及根
Hello, 90

我的五官灌满盐和语言
血滋养它们的生存，有如诗
滋养人类的虚弱，Hello

没有什么，没有铁，没有果核
没有走时准确的钟表
或其粗糙的反面

Hello, 从袖口伸出的双手
推开门的左右，道路深重
从一个年代伸入另一个

穿过双耳的疼痛穿过脑干
穿透自身的遗骸
阳光与苦难分割我的身心

松开我的手，我的牙齿
让我留在颅内的天空
留在愤怒的伤口

Hello, 有一面旗帜插在心口
有一粒种子播撒在山谷
风的去处，光阴如梭

(1990)

Hello, 90

I have not touched the other shore but I have touched
The bottom of an age, like touching the roots
Hello, 90

My five senses are filled with salt and language
Nourished by blood the same way poetry
Nourishes human weaknesses. Hello

There's nothing, no iron, no kernels
No clocks with accurate timing
Or their rough reverses

Hello, the two hands that are extended from the sleeves
Push the right and left of the door, the road deep and heavy
Going from one age to another

Through the pain of the ears, through the brains
And through the remains of the self
The sunshine and the suffering cutting up my body and heart

Let go of my hands, my teeth
Let the sky in my skull
Remain in the wound of anger

Hello, a flag is planted in the mouth of my heart
And a seed is sowed in the valley
Where the wind goes, time shuttles

(1990)

与语言同在

有一次闭门的历程远离铁轨
远离时刻
潜入原油潜入鱼鳞
潜入它的词源，听到
生锈的伤口处
牙齿绝望地生长
也听到骨骼的分化
手指的尽头涨满血液
而穿堂风是另一种语境
灯是阳光
穿透桔花的交配，雨
复活卵石复活原有的神经
最终能否明白
海水沦落成白色的盐
渗染人的灵魂
苦楝树最终越过院落
闯入意象的天空
能否明白
历尽闭门的数种劫难
等待符号成真

(1990)

Together with the Language

There was a mental process of closed doors, far away from the rails
And from time
That dove into the crude oil, the fish scales
And their etymology, hearing that
In the wound of the rust
Teeth were growing in despair
That bones were splitting apart
And that blood was swelling at the end of the fingers
While the draught formed another context
The lamp was the sunshine
Going through the copulation of orange flowers, the rain
Revived the pebbles and the original nerves
But not sure if one could in the end work out
How the sea was degraded to white salt
Infiltrating the human soul
Why the bead tree ended up crossing the courtyard
To storm into the sky of images
And why
The number of disasters after experiencing the closure of doors
Was still waiting for the symbols to come true

(1990)

流转的情怀（选一）

1.

我爱所有的一切，表象与内心
尽管结局无比沧桑
季风东奔西窜
眉目留下四季的流痕
黑暗躲在大洋彼岸，窃窃私语
思念一如既往，行动
展开羽翼的双翅
谁的内心天使般飘荡

我爱一切的所有，快乐与伤痛
尽管恩怨难解难分
风雨岁岁飘摇
血液深入不到理想的终点
阴暗侵蚀太阳的反面
感动一往情深，心智
树起一座丰碑
谁的自我时光般执着

我爱生存的幸福，平和与无奈
纵览你的善良与尖刻
我爱沉落的悲哀，美好与罪过
纵情你的顺从与反叛
我爱日月的孤寂，光明与黑暗
纵容你的任性与不羁
我爱天地的辽阔，坦荡与坎坷
纵然你的爱恨与情仇

(1990-2000)

Feelings in Circulation (Excerpt)

I love everything of all, surface and interior
Even if the end is vicissitudes, unmatched
The monsoon rushes in all directions
Leaving flow-traces of the seasons on the brows and eyes
Darkness hides itself on the other side of the ocean, whispering in private
Longing remains the same but action
Spreads its wings
Whose heart is drifting, like an angel?

I love all of everything, pleasurable and painful
Despite the inseparable entanglement of grace and rancour
Wind and rain, tottering from year to year
Blood unable to deepen into the terminal of ideals
Sombreness eroding the reverse of the sun
Feelings as deep as ever, and intelligence
Erecting a monument
Whose self is as clinging as time?

I love the happiness of existence, peaceful and helpless
Surveying your virtue and sharpness
I love the sadness of sinking, beauty and sin
Indulging in your submission and rebellion
I love the solitude of the sun and the moon, bright and dark
Pampering your wilfulness and uninhibitedness
I love the vastness of heavens and earth, broad and rugged
Despite your love and hate

(1990-2000)

我习惯于你的重量

我习惯于你的重量　习惯水
你的声音落在纸上
像极风　穿过墙基和铁

语言的光波及水一样的表面

勿需选择开始或结束
你的出现透过我的手　我的陈述
面对人类的物质和天空
呼唤另一种生存

我习惯于你的重量　习惯铁
你的手脚打开刀锋
切开河床　切开水

铁和水的反光渗入语言

勿需选择结束或开始
你的消失沉入我的心　我的变异
成就一次痛苦的美丽
以及孤独的一支笔

我习惯于你的重量　习惯物质
水是肉体　铁是心

(1991)

I'm Used to Your Weight

I'm used to your weight   used to the water
Your voice drops onto the paper
Like an extreme wind   that goes through the wall base and the iron

Lights of language, reaching the water-like surfaces, like waves

No need to choose a beginning or an end
Your appearance goes through my hand   my statement
In the face of matters of mankind and the sky
Calling for another existence

I'm used to your weight   used to the iron
Your hands and feet open the edge of a knife
Cutting open the riverbed   cutting open the water

The reflections of iron and water seeping into the language

No need to choose a beginning or an end
Your disappearance sinking into my heart   my variation
Helping achieve a painful beauty
And a solitary pen

I'm used to your weight   used to matter
Water being flesh iron being heart

(1991)

十二月的冬天

我终于躺倒在十二月的冬天　大雪纷飞
命运的车轮吞噬了一切欲望与成就
生命罪孽深重
泥土在人类面前死去
一种原始的力，重复死亡
一匹马奔驰其上

"一、二、三，去大山，
　　叫辆红色的救命车。"

邻床的病友不见血色，一身黄疸
盲眼直视的双瞳
仿佛一盏灰暗的灯，扫视海天
天光反射斜耷的脑袋
一串石头般的脚趾
一个影子从窗口跳向天国
一脸绝望的微笑

我终于躺倒在十二月的冬天　白雪茫茫
颗粒脱离麦秆而去
天才离别头颅　没有回声
生存是人类无法收获的果园
一片寂静
一只飞翔的鸟正驮起黑暗

"一、二、三，快上路，
　　接客的渡船要摇橹。"

船壳收容躯壳和邻床最后的谑语
在季节的诞生或消逝中
只有我低声歌唱
只有一位流浪的诗人
揪住自己的毛发，跋涉在江河之上
只有我的歌诵唱一个世代的腐败与更新
我终于躺倒在十二月的冬天　雪落成河

(1991)

The Winter of December

Finally, I lay down in the winter of December   a big snow flying

The wheel of fate having swallowed up all desire and achievement

Life filled with sin

Soil dying right in front of mankind

A primitive power that repeated death

Above which a horse was galloping

    'One, two, three, to the mountains

    Call a red ambulance'

The patient in the next bed was bloodless, all jaundiced

His pupils, blindly staring

Like a dim lamp, surveying the ocean and the sky in a sweeping glance

The light of the sky reflecting the head, turned askew

A string of toes, like stones

A shadow jumped to the kingdom of heaven from the mouth of the window

A smile of despair

Finally, I lay down in the winter of December   a vast snow

Grains leaving the wheat straws

Genius leaving the brain   no echoes

Existence, a garden with no human harvest

A quietness

A flying bird carrying the darkness on its back

    'One, two, three, hit the road quick

    The oars ready to row the boat'

The hull of the boat contained the hull of the body, and the last funny

words from the next bed

In the birth of the season or its vanishing

Only I was singing, in a low voice

Only a roaming poet

Grabbing hold of his own hair, trudged above the river

Only my songs chanted the corruption and renewal of an age

And, finally, I lay down in the winter of December   the snow fell, forming

a river

(1991)

女儿

穿过手术刀和等待的都市之夜
你睁着一双光刃般闪亮的眼睛
游入一方自由的天地
一对绿叶般的小手
拎进一条小溪清凉地流淌
你坐在水流之上
看见草原上的蓝天飘进来
大海伸进柔顺的触手
一颗灿烂的音乐树
挂满各色美丽的童话
在寂静的室内任意地生长
我用树的语言与你说话
用夏天的雨水把你浇灌
望着你扎根其下
像夜晚紧拉住白昼
我召唤天下所有的青鸟
落在你的树冠上放声歌唱

(1992)

46

My Daughter

Through the city night of scalpels and waiting
You, staring with a pair of eyes as shiny as the blade of light
Swam into a square of free sky and earth
And your tiny little hands, leaf-like
Carried in a creek that was coolly running
You sat above the flow
And saw the blue sky over the grassland drift in
As the ocean extended its supple tentacles
With a brilliant tree of music
From which were hanging a variety of beautiful fairy tales
Growing at random inside the quiet room
I talked to you in the tree's language
I watered you with the summer rain
Watching you take root
The way nights tightly pull the days
I called for all the green birds under heaven
To fall on your crown and burst into song

(1992)

生死之间

跨越海洋的岸跨不过最后的结局
湮灭的鱼翅沉落
生和死伸出手，海天依然辽阔
文昌鱼游到纪年的尽头
远方有树挺立，爱挂满枝头

此刻击溃太阳，无法温暖思想的躯壳
生的五指犹如一把铁锚
泊在心口，锚住最后的光明
一艘漂浮在人世的船
远得无法再近，近得无法再远

灵魂飘往何处？故乡在何方？
爱能否燃到物质的反面？

岸边的阳光照亮人类的生长
照亮紫薇花盛开的童年
岁月平整地铺展，没有波浪
彼岸是幸福各异的拥抱
不灭的灯塔守护着夜晚的航道

拒绝创造一种风格的生或死
抑或半生半死
大潮送来鱼王的声音
让灵魂脱下躯壳，告别岸的诱惑
注定孤独的孤独、苦难的苦难

灵魂飘向何处？故乡在何方？

爱能否洞穿物质的心？

(1993)

Between Life and Death

To cross the bank of the ocean was but the final finale
Fish-wings, in oblivion, were sinking
Life and death were holding out their hands although the ocean and the sky
were still vast
The Wenchang fish had swam to the end of the era
There were trees that stood erect, far in the distance, love hanging from all
the branches

This moment smashed the sun, unable to warm up the hull of thought
Five fingers of life, like an iron anchor
Were mooring at the mouth of the heart, mooring the last light
A boat drifting and floating in the world
So far one couldn't get closer and so near one couldn't get further

Where does the soul drift? Where is home?
Can love burn till it reaches the other side of matter?

The sunlight, by the bank, shines on the growth of human beings
And on the childhood blooming like jacaranda
Years spreading evenly, with no waves
The other shore but an embrace of different happinesses
The lighthouse, never extinguished, guards the passage at night

Refusing to create the life or death of a style
Or semi-life and semi-death
The great tide sends forth the voices of the fish king
Let the soul rid itself of the hull and bid farewell to the temptation of the
bank

Solitude, destined to be solitary, and suffering, destined to be suffering

Where does the soul drift? Where is home?
Can love penetrate the heart of matter?

(1993)

现状

我离开水以及它的故乡
干巴巴地，晒成一条透亮的鱼架

我把自己扔在世上
仿佛是一株等待移植的枝桠

我未能完成写作，就像
无法完成我的生命，岁岁月月

我是降临到纸上的上帝
是每一个家庭发芽的米粒

我是不灭的风，复活鸟的翅膀
是原汁，涨开麦杆之上舞动的颗粒

我也是进入思想内核的汗珠
是想象回归到火变得尖锐的地方

(1993)

The Current Situation

I have left the water and its home
Dried up, sundried into a transparent fish-frame

I have thrown myself into the world
Like a branch waiting to be transplanted

I haven't finished my writing, like
I can't complete my life, for months and years

I am God who has descended onto the paper
I am a germinating rice in every family

I am unextinguishable wind, reviving the wings of a bird
The original liquid, swelling up the grains dancing on the wheat straw

I'm also the drop of sweat that has entered into thought
And imagination that returns to the fire where it becomes sharp

(1993)

生活

大病推搡着我，向着美丽的大泽
身心发黄着脸和一双瘦削的手

心脏赶着思想，天空无比辽阔
触动日积月累的发作，触动爱与梦想

揣度一种气质，揣度自由的节拍
我邀星云一起排列字母的奥秘

天才从后脑贯向眉目，贯向爱的内部
从发根到失去痛觉的指甲

我的病痛是地球的病痛
许许多多的疾病是一个疾病

我创造鸟的语言去赞美人类
普渡生灵，让幸福不断进入身体

我掌握了一切感悟，一切痛苦
带着献身的微笑，向着人类的深渊

(1993)

Life

Serious illness is shoving me towards the beautiful marsh
Body and heart yellowing the face and a pair of thin hands

The heart chases thoughts, the sky so unmatchedly vast
That set off the breakout of accumulated years, and love and dream

Conjuring up a temperament and the rhythms of freedom
I invite the star cloud to arrange the mystery of the letters

Genius goes through the back of the brain to the brows and eyes, to the
                                                            interior of love
From the roots of hair to the fingernails no longer feeling the pain

My pain is the pain of the earth
Many an illness is one illness

I create the bird's language in praise of mankind
To deliver all living things and to let happiness enter ceaselessly into human
                                                            bodies

I master all feelings, all pain
Towards the abyss of humanity, with a devoted smile

(1993)

呓语之三

看见的飞翔是一种难以言表的秩序
季节尖锐着它们的影子
抛开结论　活力随时生存下来

群鸟的位置在于手心的批评
疲倦落在千里之外
双目的手指摸过黑暗中的流水
很早就有传说　退路一条条
翅膀的飘舞历经了颅骨所有的形式

在言语中藏起冰凉的疏忽
飞翔是一种沉静而又智性的行为
看见羽翼　看见燕尾划过的天空
单面的皮肤　流出甜甜的品味

现在明白了飞翔　在翅膀的下方
行动一些自由的目标
宽容的手放过内心的诚实　放过知觉

而在花的对面　一枝娇艳悄然无息
飘过的背景深刻在肩头
往事与理想飞来飞去
绝对的真理　软弱在现实的栏圈里

飞翔的姿势润湿水源的流逝
盛开在内部一意孤行　完善了辉煌
遥远孤独了高高低低的村落
日子挤在季节的过程中

忘却的时光　纯洁一切可爱的距离

(1993)

Raving (Part III)

Flights, when seen, are an inexpressible order

Their shadows sharpened by the seasons

As conclusions are discarded   and vitality survives any time

The position of the birds depends on the criticism in the heart of the hand

Fatigue falls beyond thousands of *li*

The fingers of the eyes have groped the currents in the dark

A legend a long time ago   the retreating path, one after another

The dancing of the wings having experienced all the shapes of the skull

With the icy neglect, hidden in the language

Flight is an act of quietness and intelligence

The wings are seen   the swallowtails that cut across the sky are seen

One-sided skin   flowing with the sweet taste

It is understood now that flight   is under the wings

Act a number of free objects

As the tolerant hands let go of the honesty inside the heart   let go of

consciousness

And, in front of the flowers   a tender beauty remains silent

The background that drifts across is profounding in the shoulders

Things of the past and ideals are flying hither and thither

Absolute truths   weakening in the stable of realities

Postures of flight moisten the flowing of the water source

Opening takes the law into its own hands inside   perfecting the brilliant

Distance lonelies the villages, high and low

Days crowd in the process of seasons

Time, forgotten   purifies all lovely distances

(1993)

我与上帝握了一下手

我与上帝握了一下手
他的手硕大无比，无所不能
我他妈的握过上帝的手
他的手苍白，透着死气
我曾向往上帝的手
一双太阳般的温暖
我想要是能握一下上帝的手
那怕轻轻的一下
我无法不握上帝的手
他的手无处不在
我无法握紧上帝的手
他的手来去无踪
我又怎敢握住上帝的手
有时却想永远握住他的手
就此了却尘世无奈愁
我似乎与上帝握了一下手
我真的握了上帝的手？
我最终握住上帝的手
他的手击中我的神经和汗孔
我与上帝握了手。没有握手。握手

(1994)

I Shook Hands with God

I shook hands with God
His hands so huge, so capable of anything
I fucking shook hands with God
I had been longing for God's hands
As warm as the sun
If only I could shake hands with God
Even if only for a gentle second
I couldn't possibly not hold God's hands
Which were omnipresent
I couldn't hold God's hands tight
As they were invisible, coming and going
How dare I shake hands with God
Although I sometimes would like to hold His hands forever
To terminate my life in this world of dust, with all my worries
I seemed to have shaken hands with God
Did I really shake hands with God?
I ended up shaking hands with God
His hands hitting my nerves and pores
I shook hands with God. Shaking. Not shaking.

(1994)

61

复活

在此辽阔的瞬间，美丽又苍茫
我独自升腾而灿烂辉煌

生之大门，敞开你黎明的眼睛
让我看看世界真实的面孔
看看今晚的世界
为了看清面包、水和空气
我一直努力向前
我蔑视人世间的死亡
书写诗行，延续有限的生命

在此辽阔的瞬间，美丽又苍茫
我独自升腾而灿烂辉煌
想象比心跳得更快
远处的山峦耸立
没有哭泣，没有悲伤
一度消退的滋润重归我的身心
新生的渴望在脉管中流淌
我的骨骼感奋火的炽热、水的喷涌
我的耳朵倾听马的嘶鸣、狮的吼叫

在此辽阔的瞬间，美丽又苍茫
我独自升腾而灿烂辉煌

风在天际间发出信号
我掀开死亡的深渊
提起伟大的青春、海浪和盐
从黑暗中分离整片光明

我是大地上自焚的火焰
穿透一切又熔化一切
我吞吃闪烁的光芒，四处飘荡

飞越时空，飞越世纪的光线
我飞过青鸟的天堂，看到生命的由来
我渡过无常河，领悟生命的意义
在此黑暗与光明交替的瞬间
我感到死神正在退缩
天空的尽头，传来一阵无限的声音
——明天，明天，明天是你的复活日！

(1994)

Resurrection

In this vast moment, beautiful and boundless
I, alone, ascend, brilliant and glorious

Entrance to life, please open your eyes of dawn
And let me see the true face of the world
The world tonight
I have been forging ahead
To clearly see the bread, the water and the air
I look down on the death in the human world
Writing poetry, prolonging the limited life

In this vast moment, beautiful and boundless
I, alone, ascend, brilliant and glorious
My imagination jumping faster than the heart
Mountains stand tall in the distance
No weeping, no saddening
Moistening, once in retreat, has now returned to my body and heart
As desire for a new life is running in my veins
My bones feeling the burning fire and erupting water
And my ears hearing the horse neighing and the lion's roaring

In this vast moment, beautiful and boundless
I, alone, ascend, brilliant and glorious

The wind is sending forth signals in the sky
As I open up the abyss of death
Lifting the great youth, sea waves and salt
Separating the whole light from the darkness

I am a fire that is burning itself to death on the land
Penetrating and melting everything
As I swallow the flashing lights, drifting all over the place

Flying across time and space, across the centennial light
I fly past the blue bird's paradise, seeing the origin of life
I cross the River of Change, appreciating the meaning of life
And, in the moment alternating with darkness and brilliance
I feel the retreat of death
From the end of the sky comes a limitless voice
—tomorrow, tomorrow, tomorrow is your day of resurrection!

(1994)

感恩

感恩的道路久久地走向远方
向东走向曙光与海洋

向北推进
草原的热烈表达我对你的感激
血在脉管中流动
苍茫从你的眼中传递
一匹美丽的马主宰这道路的漫长

我的生命
源自另一个活着的灵魂
你的世界超越所有人的高度
被黑暗围剿的田野都在向你微笑
你是我大地上灿烂盛开的花朵

你是我朝圣的目的地
巨大的峭壁远在季节之外
博爱在东方的蓝天下回荡
我的臂膀反复地生长
渴求表达感恩的真实与美好

感谢风把真情带向远方
倾听代代相传的幸福与安康

(2000)

Thanksgiving

The road to thanksgiving leads faraway, for a long, long time
Eastwards to dawn and ocean

Pushing north
The passion of the grassland expresses my gratitude to you
The blood is running in the veins
Vastness is being conveyed in your eyes
A beautiful horse reigns over the length of this road

My life
Originates from another living soul
Your world goes beyond the height of everyone
The fields, encircled by darkness, are smiling for you
And you are the flower that is brilliantly blooming in my land

You are the destination of my pilgrimage
The enormous cliffs are so far they are outside the seasons
Universal love is reverberating under the blue skies of the Orient
My arms repeatedly grow
Desiring to express the genuineness and beauty of thanksgiving

Thank the wind for carrying true feelings faraway
Listening to the happiness and wellbeing, from generation to generation

(2000)

黑陶

就像我全部的经历
烧制的语言是我透彻
生存的想象力
沉淀在流动的核心。纹饰与色泽
只是附属世界的牺牲品
时光一代代谋杀躯体
谁又能谋杀黑陶内部的宁静
成功只是散落的瓦砾
铺开阳光下无限延伸的背景
陶片的心情是黑色的斑点
落笔的余晖在于多年的颠沛与腕力
未来是一座铺满盐的岛屿
生活的浪升上来，夹带着鱼
就像我一次次的努力
风坍下去，彷佛整座墙
清晨的伤口塞满指节、花与泪
黑陶口涂抹的汗水
涌动人类原初的想象与祝福

(2000)

Black Pottery

Like all my experience

The language, burned, is the imaginative

power of my thorough existence

Depositing in the core of flowing. The emblazonry and the tinctures

Are but the victims of a world of accessories

Time murders bodies, generation after generation

But who can murder the stillness inside the black pottery?

Success is but the scattered rubble

That spreads the unlimited extension of the background under the sun

The mood of the pottery is the black spots

And the evening glow where the pen is put down depends on years'

hardships and wrist-power

Future is an island covered in salt

When waves of life ascend, carrying fish in them

Like my multiple efforts

The wind collapses, like a wall

The wound of the morning is filled with knuckles, flowers and tears

The sweat smeared over the mouth of the black pottery

Is surging with the original imagination and goodwill of mankind

(2000)

失落的技艺

我丢失了一门技艺，说难也不难
那么多东西注定要失落
失去一些，也许真的没有什么

每天都在丢失。丢失房门的钥匙
虚度了年华，思索起怨屈
最终失去原则，坚持那么多年

丢弃相伴的老怀表，就在一瞬间
沧桑爬上额头、眼角与眉梢
我错失找寻的良机，内心无法挽留

我丢失的技艺也不难恢复
当初是水到渠成，也就一瞬间
重要是寻找恢复的信心

我丢失相守的热土和一片森林
二条相汇的河流
失去它们，也许真的没有什么

我丢失了幸福，话题无从说起
舌头垂落在嘴角的内侧
失去兴奋的理由，更不必说明

我甚至丢失了你，声音与眼光
那么的喜欢，哪怕谎言
这一次的失落不知是福还是祸？

(2001)

The Lost Craft

I've lost a craft. It's easy and not easy
So many things are destined for loss
So, it really doesn't matter if some does get lost

Making a loss daily. Losing the key to the door of the house
Losing years, and one thinks of rancour
How one has lost one's principle after sticking to it for so many years

Losing the companion, the old pocket watch, and in a brief moment
Weathering has crept onto the brow, the corner of the eye and the tip of the brow
I've lost the opportunity to search, nothing to retain at heart

It's easy to recover the craft I've lost
As it was achieved, in a moment, effortlessly back then
The important thing is to look for the recovered confidence

I've lost the hot earth and a spread of forest in company
Two converging rivers
Perhaps, it really is nothing to lose them

I've lost happiness, a topic I can't even begin talking about
My tongue dropped to the inside of the corner of my mouth
I've lost my reason for excitement, something unnecessary to explain

I've even lost you, your voice and the way you look
I liked you so much, even if your lies
Is this loss a disaster or something to be happy about?

(2001)

71

坎大哈

一个逃亡的女人穿越沙漠
她要去坎大哈
拯救一个濒死的灵魂

沟壑之上，黑色的落日悬空
无人知晓
她能否到达目的地
是否有足够的时光抵达内心

自由的旗，飘在破车的一角
诚实的布加遮掩一切
死亡近在咫尺

沙漠深处，阿訇的经诵传来
别哭，真主宽恕一切
赐予我们所有
他浓密的胡子向下，直抵恐惧

一个孤独的女人正穿越沙漠
哭泣的骆驼
给她一个坚持下去的理由

(2001，选自组诗《家园》)

Kandahar

An escaping woman went through the desert
On her way to Kandahar
To save a dying soul

Over the ravines, the black setting sun was suspended
No one knew
If she could reach the destination
Or if she had enough time to reach the heart of hearts

The flag of freedom, flapping in a corner of the broken-down vehicle
And the honest burqa concealed everything
While death was near at hand

In the depths of the desert, came Imam's chanting
Don't cry as Allah forgives all
And blesses us all
His dense moustache, pointing downwards, directly reaches fear

A lonely woman was walking across the desert
And the crying camel
Gave her a reason for persistence

(2001, selected from my sequence, *Homeland*)

南波希米亚的红瓦顶

越过波希米亚的那片丛林
向南延伸，再向南
一座红瓦顶，成片的红瓦顶明亮
蓝色多瑙河静静地流淌
穿越整个大陆，穿越时光

到达那片土地，并不十分艰难
只需点滴的努力
而瞭望南方的尽头，直达
古希腊文明，远非
简单地搭乘一趟午夜的班机

波希米亚，翻飞想象的翅翼
晶莹的水晶闪亮，思想
尽情地放浪，先锋或浪漫
一条河，一座城市
从左岸到右岸

一片浸染阳光的红瓦顶
越过几片松林，流水蜿蜒而行
一束波希米亚的光亮
刺破黑夜，浸润生活的平淡
波及布波一族，波及自由的心灵

(2002)

74

The Red Rooftiles in Southern Bohemia

Across the bush in Bohemia
Towards the south, further south
A building of red rooftiles, spreads of bright red rooftiles
Where the blue Danube is quietly running
Across the continent, and through time

It's not hard to reach that land
You only have to make a bit of an effort
But if you want to see the end of the south and to reach
Ancient Greek civilization, it's not as
Simple as riding an airplane at midnight

Bohemia, where wings of imagination take flight
Sparkling crystal is shining, thinking
Goes unrestrained, avant-garde or romantic
A river, a city
From the left bank to the right

A spread of red rooftiles dyed in sunlight
Across the pine forests, flowing waters are meandering
A bunch of Bohemian lights
Pierce the darkness and moisten the vapidity of life
Reaching, like waves, the bobos and the free hearts and souls

(2002)

夜莺

夜莺，飞翔在城市的上空
一切料理停当。此刻无奈
单向行驶的生命
停在走廊尽头
呼吸机撤在一旁，气管外露
非典病毒不再出入
忙碌的天使，直起了腰

夜莺，飞越烟消云灭的战场
南丁格尔，提着一盏油灯前行
微弱的光透过恐惧
温暖破碎的心，一代又一代
一丝安宁随手指滑落
从垂闭的眼睑
从银幕复活远去的记忆

夜莺，飞翔在生死的界限
人间天使，一身白色防护服
一双黑眼睛，双十字闪亮
勇气穿透疾病与苦难
白昼追击黑夜
献身与幸福同行
爱心与生命紧紧相随

(2003)

76

The Nightingale

The nightingale is flying over the city

With everything ready. Helpless at this very moment

Life that is traveling one way

Has come to a stop at the end of the corridor

The respirator, left to the side, its trachea exposed

So that the SARS virus is no longer able to enter or exit

And the busy angels are straightening themselves up

The nightingale is flying across the battlefield where the cloud has
disappeared

Nightingale is walking forward, an oil lamp in hand

The dim light through the fear

And a warm broken heart, generation after generation

A thread of peace and quiet slips from the fingers

While memory moving far away is revived from the closed eyelids

And from the movies

The nightingale is flying in the boundary between life and death

A human angel, in a white protection uniform

A pair of black eyes, a shiny double-cross

Whose courage penetrates the disease and misery

The day chasing the night

Devotion walking together with happiness

A loving heart close on the heels of life

(2003)

心火

捐出一颗心，捐出
你的高贵、仁慈与美丽
献出一份爱心，消除病痛
茫茫人海，生命如此的熟悉

心与心紧紧相随
另一种亲情凝固同一片星空
心形的火焰刺破夜色
幸福广场辽阔无限

搏动的一颗心，两颗心……
从西方传向东方
从海洋回涌江河与大地
心火不灭，生命永不停息！

(2003)

The Fire in the Heart

Donate a heart, donate

Your nobility, your kindness and beauty

Give a loving heart and remove the conditions

Life, so familiar, in a sea of people

Heart follows heart, closely

Another kind of familial love is solidified in the same sky of stars

As the heart-shaped fire pierces the colours of the night

And the square of happiness remains vast and boundless

A leaping heart, two hearts…

From the West to the East

Surging from the ocean back to the rivers and the land

The heart-fire unextinguishable, and life unstoppable!

(2003)

红丝带

红丝带终于浮出水面
泪流向丝线的两端，不留痕迹

危机，讳莫如深的字眼
更兼 AIDS 蕴涵隐喻
渴望的生灵，漠然的天空
打破沉默的坚冰
需要付出多大的勇气？

红丝带飘过欲望的街口
夜幕下的交易，病毒肆意狂欢
吸毒嫖妓同性恋，哪怕一夜情
上帝也设定危险的系数
自然的法则维系生态的平衡

红丝带飘落在中原的坟地
孤儿们睁大眼，略带些恐惧
目送一位慈祥的姥姥走出风雨
上帝，为何要惩罚那些无辜的人
就因为他们的愚昧与无知？

再次侧耳倾听
丝带在风中飘动的声音
HIV 离我们越来越近
哦，红丝带！
飘摇的心灵该如何传递你的美丽？

(2004)

The Red Ribbon

The red ribbon, finally emerging out of the water
With tears running towards its ends, leaving no traces

A crisis, a carefully avoided word
With AIDS rich with metaphor
The desirous life, the indifferent skies
How much courage is needed
To break the ice?

The red ribbon drifts across the street junction of desire
Trading under cover of the night when viruses are wildly carnivalistic
Taking drugs, visiting whores, going gay, but even for a one-night stand
God sets a risk factor
And natural rules maintain an ecological balance

The red ribbon falls drifting down on the graves of the Central Plains
Where orphans open their eyes wide, slightly with fear
Watching a kindly granny walk out of the wind and rain
God, why punish the innocent people
Just because of their stupidity and ignorance?

Let me listen, once again, to
The fluttering sound of the red ribbon in the wind
As HIV is getting closer to us
Oh, the red ribbon
How will the shaking heart and soul convey your beauty?

(2004)

村落

揭开地表下的秘密，一层又一层
泥土与稻种、陶与罐
明与暗沉睡其间
窥探的一挖，漏了光
究竟是靠近地狱还是抵达天堂

一根根木桩，绵延状刺向天空
几乎碳化，却拒绝风化
干栏撑起一处遗迹
只有梦境轻松地穿越时光
穿越物质自身的死亡

曾经的枝叶扛起冬天的大雪
更兼春花又秋月
场景倾斜向下，再向下
历史的火终究无法彻底熄灭
一枚燧石，随时点燃黑暗的灵魂

年复一年的绿意，生长在地面
目光消散之前
或许不仅仅是一种凭吊
风尽量地放低风度，与生活默契
谁会改变一个村落的意义

The Village

When you reveal the secrets below the crust of the earth, layer by layer
Light and dark are asleep amongst
Mud and rice seeds, pottery and earthenware
A peeking dig leaks the light
And one wonders if he is getting close to hell or has reached heaven

Wooden pillars, one by one, continuously poke into the sky
Refusing to be decomposed although almost carbonized
Where the railings hold up a relic
Only dreams can easily go through time
Through the death of matter itself

The erstwhile branches and leaves shoulder the big snow of the winter
Past the spring flowers and the autumn moon
The scene inclines downwards, further downwards
But the fire of history, after all, refuses to be thoroughly extinguished
And a flint can set fire to the dark soul any time

The greenness, year in, year out, grows on the ground
Before the vision disappears
Or it's not a mere visit
As the wind tries hard to lower its degree in reaching a tacit understanding
                                                                with life
Who will want to change the meaning of a village?

偶婚

一个汉子，奔涉在沼泽之上
春暖花又开，雪已融
一次次黄昏的行程
在幽暗的密林抵达他的使命

一方干栏之上
风抽动腔内的哨棒
哨音散开来，一枝竹叶悠扬
榫头与卯孔，耙耕劳作
雨水浇灌一个季节的所有过程

一场刀耕火种的颤动
一次痉挛的起伏
流水啊流水，欲望游历其中

黑夜，一再遮掩聆听的地平线
手脚读懂姿势里的奔腾
无花果垂下身，谷穗隐了形
一道光穿越天空下的翅膀
白昼跟随而来，从此有了生命

一个女子，深居在村落中心
青草、鸟鸣、水罐
偶婚的日子简单又浅出
一片自由的断层掩没她的尊严

Paired Marriage

A man is trudging on a marshland
Where the spring is warm with opening flowers, and the snow is melting
Trips at dusk, one after another
And he arrives at his mission in the gloomy dense forest

Above the railing
The wind draws out the whistle from inside the body
As the whistle spreads, a branch of bamboo leaves becomes melodious
All but tenon-and-mortise work, sheer *si*-ploughing farm work
As the rain is watering the whole process of a season

A trembling cultivation by slashing and burning
A heaving of convulsions
Flowing waters, ah, flowing waters, with desire swimming in them

Dark night keeps covering it from the listening horizon
As hands and feet can understand the rushing in the gestures
Figs lower themselves and grain ears render themselves invisible
A shaft of light penetrates the wings in the sky
And, with the coming of the day, a life is born

A woman, deeply living in the centre of the village
With green grass, birdsong, water jars
Days of paired marriage are simple and shallow
And a fault of freedom covers her dignity

传说

风骤起于史前，一次偶然的编配
心海泛滥，雨花层层叠叠
口舌触摸词语的痕迹
嘴张大表情，找寻某些空位
最终达成虚设的意念

遥远的水流变换方向
言而不尽的事物
就此一点一滴地在湖泊显现
向南翻过山，再趟过河
鲜活的话语最终逼近海水的边界

火焰刻在木纹之上
一次就能照亮被遮蔽的黑暗
诞生的村庄，虚构的院落
置身其中，生根或发芽
故事渐渐变得具体又抽象

为虚无生存的一套传说
看见飞鸟倾泄月光
声音穿透一切
肺腑之言抵达一时的恐惧
河水洗涤幸福的内涵

言语遭遇一番激情
欲说还休，想象一再深入底线
终将黄墓渡说成河姆渡
七千年的文化沉甸甸

灵与肉的界限，终将难解难分

(2004，以上三首选自组诗《江南·河姆渡》)

A Legend

The wind suddenly rose prior to history as the result of an accidental
arrangement
When the ocean of the heart flooded and flowers of rain became layered
The tongue touched the traces of words
And the mouth, agape, searched for the empty seats
Finally reaching a nominal idea

The distant waterflow changed its direction
And things, that defied expressing
Revealed themselves, bit by bit, in the lakes
If one goes south by climbing the mountain and crossing the river
Fresh language will finally get close to the boundary of the sea

When the flame is carved in the grains of the wood
It will light up the concealed darkness in one go
The village born and the courtyard fictionalised
When you are in them, striking roots or geminating
The story will become concrete and abstract

A set of legends, for the existence of nothingness
Sees the birds pour the moonlight
The sound penetrates all
Words from the bottom of one's heart reaches an occasional fear
While the river water washes the contents of happiness

When speech encounters passion
There's no more point talking about it for imagination gets deeper into the
bottomline

Finally describing the Huangmu Du as the Hemudu

In this heavy culture of seven thousand years

It won't be easy to distinguish between body and soul

(2004, the three poems above are selected from the sequence, *River South·Hemudu*)

长椅

游人罕见的山岗，东临辽阔的大西洋
置放一把长椅，又一把
如果斜坡再陡一些
如果山脚下的草皮再延伸一些
椅子的摆放会更悠闲从容

圆圆的地球，海水自由地流动
天空划下一个优美的弧
涂抹岁月的流逝

一把长椅纪念亲人的长眠
此刻无人歇坐
防雨漆黯然
风在背后任意地吹动

我独自抚摸椅背上的铜牌
看着，看着
一枚高尔夫球
从虚无的画面飞出
又一道自然的弧度，翻越宁静的气流

(2005)

The Bench

On a mountain ridge, with few people, facing the vast Atlantic Ocean in the

East

A bench was placed, then another
If the slope was steeper
And if the turf was more extensive
The positioning of the benches would have been more relaxed

On the round earth, the waters of the ocean were freely flowing
And the sky drew a beautiful curve downwards
Smearing the years with their lapse

A bench was a memorial to the long sleep of the beloved
No one rested on it at the moment
The rain-proof paint downcast
And the wind blew behind it at will

Alone, I was touching the bronze plate on the back of the bench
As I looked and looked
A golf ball
Flew out of the painting of nihility
In another natural curve that climbed over the air currents

(2005)

访谈

黑夜或白昼
听到与人访谈的话语
活跃在口舌之上
真诚或圆滑
声音撑开语言的外壳
最终干枯在纸面
话筒之后的半张脸
表情起伏不定
意识常常从嘴角走失
手足不知所措
一种内在的声响
隔着重重叠叠的屋顶
在另一片天际回响
虚设的意义呈现
空洞或充实
场景销声匿迹
话筒一次次追击话语
天南地北
访谈仍在继续
思想却越走越远

The Interview

By night or day

I heard the words in an interview with someone

Active on the tongue

Sincere or tongue in cheek

The voice expanding the shell of language

Till it withered on the face of the page

The expressions heaving

On the half-face behind the microphone

As consciousness often went missing at the corner of the mouth

And hands and feet were bewildered

An inner voice

Kept from the layered roofs

Was resounding in another sky

Meaning, in name only, revealed itself

Hollow or substantial

When the real scene vanished without a trace

The microphone kept chasing after the discourse

In all directions

While the interview was continuing

Thoughts went further away

词句

词是道路，句在道路上行走
生存或死亡
谁在倾听语言的游戏？

名词远离时间的流动
寻找句子中的物像
流水依旧
动词磕磕碰碰
字符成螺旋形翻转
美好再生邪恶
一道闪电击中万物的象征

声音，随时因人而异
意义无关对与错
起风了下雨了
有人关闭了所有的门窗
有人开启了所有的通道
颂词与咒语
在一个句子中生成或替换

词是道路，句在道路上行走
随意或严谨
破碎的词比完整的句子更富想象

Words and Sentences

Words are roads and sentences travel on them
To live or to die
Who's listening to the play of language?

Nouns are keeping a distance from the flow of time
While looking for the images of the sentences
Running waters remain the same
But verbs stumble along
Characters turning over in a spiral format
Beauty re-breeding evil
In a lightning that hits the symbol of all things

Voices differ from one person to another
Meaning has nothing to do with either right or wrong
The wind is rising and the rain is raining
Someone has closed all the doors and windows
And someone has opened all the passageways
Eulogies and curses
Are generated or replaced in a single sentence

Words are roads and sentences travel on the roads
Casually or strictly
The broken words are more imaginative than complete sentences

镜像

一行行镜中反向的文字
上下错落有致
光芒在夜里独自生长
明亮的一侧是无尽的黑暗

东方与西方
左岸或右倾
声音的外壳反向呈现
极乐的无常是幻灭的反光

残缺的笔划，空缺的字母
失语后遗留的黑白镜像
闪烁思维的痕迹
图像的天窗说白了复杂的道

诉说的水汽弥漫开来
淹没了平滑的镜面
思想，流畅或笨拙的
徒然间迷离，遁入无形

时光无所不在
伸出弯曲的手指
试图触摸镜面里的身体
虚狂的恐惧撕开扁平的头颅

(2006，以上三首选自组诗《镜像》)

Mirror Images

Rows of words in reverse in a mirror

Evenly placed up and down

Lights grow alone at night

Boundless darkness to the side of the brightness

East and West

Left Bank or rightist

The shell of sound is revealed in reverse

 And the inconstance of extreme pleasure is the reflection of disillusionment

Incomplete strokes and the missing letters

Black and white mirror images after the loss of the language

Traces of flashing thoughts

The skylight of images has said it all about the complex Tao

The steam of the narration is suffusing

Drowning the smooth mirror surface

Thoughts, flowy or clumsy

Become blurred, in a vain moment, disappearing into the invisibility

Time, omnipresent

Holds out with bent fingers

In an attempt to touch the body in the mirror surface

As the mad fear is tearing the flat head apart

(2006, the three poems above are selected from a sequence, titled, *The Mirror Images*)

奥赫里德湖

奥赫里德湖惊起的一片羽叶
一路行云流水
岸边的芦苇轻轻摇曳
诗情盎然，感动悄然打湿了心意

诗屋之门打开
火把洞穿夜的黑
仿佛一朵朵爆开的礼花
我置身其中，汉语亦置身其中

瓦达尔河畔。一株丁香花盛开
风信子开满戈提尼雅山
废墟之上，亚力山大柱耸立
陶罐的碎片撒满文化的伤口

蚂蚁们列队爬上修道院豁口
在历史的壶沿进进出出
野菊开满山岗
风景随野草一路疯长

奥赫里德湖诗桥的一股清泉
随流云在岁月间逍遥
无意间，我千里迢迢穿越帝国
生长的诗路，早已翻越了千山万水

(2009，第48届马其顿斯特鲁加国际诗歌节)

The Ohrid Lake

The feather of a leaf, stirred up on the Ohrid Lake
Goes on its way, natural and spontaneous
The reeds on the bank gently sway
With an abundant sense of poetry while my heart is quietly moved, moistened

The door is opened to the house of poetry
And the fire crashes through the darkness of the night
Like the blasting fireworks amidst which
I find myself and the Chinese language also finds itself

On the bank of the Vardar River, a lilac is in full bloom
The Gortynia Mountain covered with hyacinth
Towering over the ruins, stands the Alexander Column
The cultural wounds are scattered all over the fragments of pottery

The ants, in a single file, are climbing onto the gap of the monastery
In and out of the edge of the pot in history
Wild chrysanthemums fill the ridge
As the landscape goes wild all the way with the feral grass

A clean spring at the Bridge of Poetry on the Ohrid River
Happily wanders amidst the years along with the clouds
Inadvertently, I have covered thousands of miles and gone through the empire
And the poetry road of growth has long climbed over thousands of
mountains and waters

(2009, written at the 48th International Poetry Festival in Struga,
Macedonian)

飞翔

一架战斗机的起飞，紧贴着村庄
呼啸声穿越海天
穿越了童年

一架客机的降落，紧贴着小区
比小鸟飞得更低
比记忆更深入

一架大型客机的飞翔，紧贴着城市
上上下下，世界
从此越来越大，又越来越小

(2010)

Flight

A fighter plane took flight, close to the village
Its roaring across the sky and the sea
Through childhood

The descending of a passenger plane, close to the Small District
Lower than the birds
Lower, than memory

The flight of a large-sized passenger plane, close to the city
Up and down as the world
Is getting bigger and bigger, then smaller and smaller

(2010)

暮色

暮冬，落叶飘入颓败的院落
光秃秃的树无声
乡野一览无遗
除了一茬茬稻桩，齐崭崭的
仰望炊烟缓缓飘过村落
落日的缕缕余晖
斜倚在冰冷的石凳上
无意涂抹一旁盛开的腊梅
院落之外，池塘泛起几分落寞
一圈又一圈
对岸的竹林，风骤起
忽啦啦，吹落归乡人一脸的尘土
却吹不散一方的乡音
更远处，乡野的天际辽阔
夕阳静静地移动
融入更深更浓的夜色

(2010)

At Dusk

Late winter, when fallen leaves fall drifting into the courtyard in ruins

The bare trees soundless

The country in full view

Except for the even rice stubbles, in neat order

Raising their heads to watch the chimney smoke sluggishly drifting across

the village

Wisps of the remaining glow of the setting sun

Are leaning against the icy-cold stone bench

Unintentionally smearing the wintersweet to the side

Outside the courtyard, the pond ripples with parts of solitude

Ring after ring

In the bamboo forest from across the river, the wind suddenly rises

With a whooping noise, blowing the dust off the returnee's face

But not the village sound that comes from the square of a place

Further away, in the vastness of the fields

The setting sun moves, quietly

Merging into the deeper and thicker colours of the night

(2010)

雪夜

未等静下心来怀念旧岁，多事之秋
已远去，冬夜深处，飞雪
仿佛一场纷乱的心情

飞鸽，一群飞翔的羽翼
为风雪所歇
一脉细流依然努力向大海

又一年流逝，雪夜无眠
村庄忙于祭祖、祈望
失地的乡下人，仿佛
干裂的冻土，感觉不到痛

深夜，雪意渐浓
村后蜿蜒的小河不停地流
村前一角，稻垛们
在飞雪中遥望更白更亮的新岁

(2010)

The Snowy Night

I hadn't waited to calm myself down to miss the old year when the eventful
autumn
Had gone. In the depths of the winter night, the flying snow
Seemed in a messy mood

The flying doves were a group of flying wings
Were resting, on account of the wind and snow
  Although a trickle of fine flow was still making an effort towards the ocean

Another year gone and sleepless on the snowy night
The village was busy paying respects to the ancestors and praying
The villagers, with their land lost, like
The cracked frozen earth, felt no pain

Late at night when the snow deepened
The small meandering river behind the village kept flowing
In a corner in front of the village, sheaves of rice straw
Were watching a whiter and brighter new year in the flying snow

(2010)

怀念

怀念是一抹淡淡的忧伤
抹不去，道不明
沉积在血脉里
三月的樱花已谢
四月的菜地吐出了新芽

怀念是一阵阵痛的喜悦
说不尽，道不明
闪烁在眉梢
七月的流火未落
八月的酷热难耐

怀念成一种解脱的宁静
散发出迷人的芳香
水鸭在河塘漫步
苍鹭在水面滑翔
十月的叶子红透了
秋意一泻千里

怀念凝成一幅窗景的美丽
晚归的小车熄了火
挥不去的家园
萦绕在心灵
冬日的阳光好温暖
十二月的大雪依然纷飞

我怀念往日的时光，岁岁月月
我流连失落的光阴，分分秒秒

(2013)

Yearning

Unerasable and unspeakable
Yearning is a light sorrow
That sediments in the blood veins
When the cherries of March have shed
And vegetable plots of April are budding

Unspeakable and unsayable
Yearning is pangs of painful delight
That flicker on the brow
When the flow-fire in July hasn't dropped
And the scorching heat of August is unendurable

Yearning till it becomes the stillness of a disentanglement
That sends forth attractive aromas
Ducks are walking on the river-pond
Herons glide over the water
Leaves are red through and through in October
And the feel of the autumn rushes along for thousands of *li*

Yearning congeals in a beautiful window scene
When the car, coming home late, stalls
And the unforgettable home garden
Encircles the heart
The sunshine is so warm on the winter day
Although the big snow in December still flies around

I yearn for the past time, months and years
And I linger on the lost time, seconds and minutes

(2013)

出离

一切都会过去
一切都不必太在意
一转身也许就到了尽头

菩提是棵永恒的树，忘了忧伤
唯有放下俗念
空下的双手才能拾起幸福

尘世如云烟而逝
出离何尝不是一种领悟
心境如诗如画

一切早已有了答案
与其逆风烦扰
不如顺风穿过了流沙

赶自己的路，看一个人的风暴
唯有到了终点，才明白旅途的意义

(2014)

Nissarana

We'll go past everything
It's not necessary to mind anything
When you turn around you may have reached the end

Linden is an eternal tree, forgetful of the sorrow
Only by laying down the secular thoughts
Can the disengaged hands pick up happiness

The dusty world will die like clouds and smoke
Isn't leaving an insight of sorts
When the state of mind resembles poetry and painting?

There's an answer to everything
Rather than trouble oneself against the wind
One ought to go through the flowing sands with the wind

Hurry on your own way and watch the storm of one person
Only when you arrive at the end can you understand the meaning of the
journey

(2014)

废墟里的玫瑰

一粒麦子，若不落在地里死去
来春就难再现麦芒的落花
不历经掩埋，怎能重获生的旨意

一枝风信子，吐出蓝色的花蕊
只因有位石匠选择了死去
他说不愿去雕刻一幅异教徒的画像

一粒芥菜子，种在园子长成一棵树
天上的飞鸟赶来栖息在枝头
盼望的信心就随芥菜种日夜长大

一颗无花果，藏满了智慧的奇迹
一副宽大的叶片是一件奇异的衣裳
谁梦见无花果，就走进了一片伊甸园

一棵葡萄树，缠满可结果子的藤蔓
你在里面我在里面她在里面
离开了沙仑，玫瑰依然是美丽的玫瑰

一座教堂，一座修道院
旷野和干旱之地必得欢喜
废墟那残灰落处，回声腾起生机
荆棘间几朵百合随之散发出花香

(2016)

Roses in the Ruins

A grain of wheat, if it does not drop and die in the earth
Will find it hard to re-exhibit the fallen flowers on the awns next spring
If it is not buried, how can it regain the meaning of regeneration?

A hyacinth spits out a blue pistil
Only because a stonemason has chosen to die
Saying he won't carve the picture of a heathen

A mustard seed has grown into a tree in the garden
In which the flying birds in the sky hurry to dwell
And the confidence in longing grows, day and night, with the mustard seed

A fig hides the miracle of wisdom
A broad leaf is a piece of strange clothing
Whoever dreams of the fig will walk into an Eden

A grapevine is tangled with vines capable of bearing fruit
You are in them, I'm in them, she's in them
When leaving Sharon, roses are still beautiful roses

A church and a monastery
The wilderness and the arid land must be delighted
Where residual ashes fall in the ruins, echoes rise with vitality
And amongst the thorns, lilacs emanate fragrances forthwith

(2016)

隋梅

隋塔下，梅亭旁
听法师拈一枝梅花，心就溢满花香
1400 年前，也许更早些
浙东一支水系出钱塘
沿剡溪溯流南下上青山
问我何处去，又到天台看石梁
少时敢打梁上行，却不敢俯瞰深潭
茂密竹林间，一泓飞瀑梁下落

寺既成，国乃清
法师植下一株梅，朝夕闻晨钟暮鼓
智者"一念三千"天台宗
捕捉一念心起，你我诗意足矣
寒山与拾得终成就和合文化
"世间谤我、欺我、辱我、笑我、轻我、贱我、恶我、骗我，该如
　　　　　　　　　　　　　　　　　何处之乎？"
"只需忍他、让他、由他、避他、耐他、敬他、不要理他，再待几
　　　　　　　　　　　　　　　年，你且看他。"
24 首寒山诗竟成为异国不朽经典

山门外，古道边
一行到此水西流，高山杜鹃尚早
竞演诗人杖藜行歌山水间
院庭内，坐看满目萧瑟
唯有一树白梅早春花满枝
踏遍青山，停不下前行的脚步
同题"隋梅"比拼三十年自我

且随花香，穷尽浙东唐诗路迢迢

(2018)

The Wintersweet of the Sui Dynasty

Under the Sui Pagoda and by the side of the Wintersweet Pavilion
When I listened to the Buddhist master picking up a branch of wintersweet,
my heart was filled with flowery fragrance
1400 years ago or earlier
A river in East Zhejiang ran out of Qiantang
Southward along the Shan River till it went up the green hills
If you ask where I went, I went to Tiantai to see the Stone Beam
When young, I dared walk on the beam but I didn't dare look down on the
deep pool
In the dense bamboo forest, a flying cascade fell down the beam

When the temple was built and the nation was cleared off
The master planted a wintersweet, and he heard the morning bells and
evening drumbeats
'A thought, three thousand'[1] for the intelligent, in the Tiantai denomination
The catch done with the rise of a thought when you and I have enough
poetry
Han Shan and Shi De combine to make a culture of harmony
'How can I deal with people who abuse me, bully me, insult me, laugh at
me, belittle me, disgust me and deceive me?'
'Bear him, let him, up to him, avoid him, endure him, respect him, ignore
him before you look at him in a few years'
24 poems by Han Shan have become immortal classics overseas

---

1   "A thought, three thousand" （一念三千）, an important Buddhist principle of
Tiantai denomination, is derived from the Great Concentration and Insight （智顗：《摩
诃止观》）, created by the Master Zhiyi (538-597) in the Sui dynasty, meaning that
our mind or attitude in a single moment of life can change everything.

Outside the mountain gate and by the side of the ancient road

Master Yi Xing arrived here where the water runs west, and it's still early

days for the mountain rhododendron

Actually poets, with walking sticks, walk as they sing, among the mountains

and waters

And, in the courtyard, they sit and watch the bleakness that fills their eyes

Except a tree of white wintersweet in full early spring bloom

When they walk around the green hills they find their steps unstoppable

Competing with each other writing poems under the same title of 'The

wintersweet of the Sui Dynasty' for thirty years

They take the long poetry journey of the Tang dynasty in East Zhejiang,

along with the fragrance of the flowers

(2018)

山中晓望

天台邻四明，华顶高百越。
门标赤城霞，楼栖沧岛月。

——李白《天台晓望》

山间的寒露更深了，云雾更重
看不尽隔窗的秋叶飘零
纵然山呑掩映半轮夕阳
纵然山南初露一丝晨光

昨夜梦江帆、闻木叶，冷风习习
今日已抵大竹园福溪的尽头
仆船码头空悬铭牌一枚
覆舟于岸，不忘赋诗一首

遥想当年诗人远航东南望
青山绿水烂漫四野
丹霞映红天际
古朴旧祠说不尽沧海桑田

一曲天台高腔竹园调
风敲起竹板，惊起北雁东南飞
一首道情应和浙东唐诗之路和合行
云霞明灭，回荡内心的山水与远方

(2018)

Watching at Daybreak in the Mountain

The Tiantai Mountain neighbours the Siming Mountain
And the Huading Peak stands above the Baiyue.
The red glow is the symbol of the Chicheng Mountain
While the moon of the Cangdao Island likes to rest on its pagoda.

From 'Watching at the Daybreak in Tiantai' by Li Bai

The cold dew is deeper in the mountain and the cloudy haze, heavier
I can't see the fading of the autumnal leaves outside the window
Even if the valley half conceals a setting sun
And a thread of morning light is shown on the southern side of the mountain

Last night, I dreamed of the river sails, heard the leaves in the wood, with
cold wind
By today I've reached the end of Happy Creek in Big Bamboo Garden
Where, at the pier, an empty nameplate was hanging
When the poet arrived there, overturning his boat, he wouldn't forget to
write a poem

I recalled how the poet, in their days, went far in their boats south-eastwards
And watched the green hills and waters, and the blooming fields
The red morning or evening glow painting the sky red
And the simple ancient temples couldn't possibly relate their sea changes

In a high-pitched tune of bamboo garden, Tiantai-style
The wind knocks on the bamboo clappers, surprising the northern swans
that fly southeast
A Daoqing ballad echoing the joined poetry journey of the Tang dynasty in

117

East Zhejiang

When the clouds and glows shine and go out, reverberating with the
mountains and waters in the heart of hearts and the faraway

(2018)

良渚·玉鸟

热衷于飞翔，想象比风更流畅
鸟纹抽象翅膀所有的演化
浮尘岂能遮蔽一路的飞扬
玉鸟，立于时光之上
火焰从视毛孔渗入窥探者的内心

沙洲北岸不见人流，唯有远山如黛
江河的源头是一片水泽
打磨石器时代断代与否的交替
斜坡撒满陶片，盛开漫山的黄秋英
墓地深处垒起一垄信仰的祭石

濯洗的祭坛，露水自然地滑落
鸟的迁涉，打开一部史前的传说
所有的部落隐身于尘埃
荒草举着火苗，烧过待耕的田野
陶罐内，笑声一浪更比一浪高

真知或谎言，开始与结束
内心感知天际间的一道道闪电
流失的思绪蓦然回返
水在泥土间预设离席的裂隙
远方西斜，日子终究遗落在一旁

瑶山，群鸟翔集五千年
祭坛的鼓声远去，隔着三重土色
云烟有意，流水终究无痕
一对圆睁的眼神，传递神灵的飞翔

美丽洲升腾文明曙光，两岸惟有苍茫

(2018)

Liangzhu - Jade Birds

They are passionate about flight, their imagination smoother than the wind
The bird veins abstracting all the evolution of the wings
How can the floating dust conceal the flying all the way through?
The jade birds stand above time
The flame seeping into the inner heart of the voyeur via the viewing pores

No crowds are seen on the northern bank of the sandbar except the distant
dark hills
The source of the rivers is a water plain
Whether or not the alternate Stone Age is polished in the division of history
into periods
The slope is covered with pieces of pottery and the hills, the yellow cosmos
In the depths of the graveyard is built a ridge of sacrificial stone of faith

Dew water naturally falls off the washed altar
The migration of birds opens up a pre-historic legend
All the tribes hide themselves in the dust
The wild grass holds up flames, having burnt the fields waiting for farming
Inside the pots, waves of laughter, one higher than the other

Truth or lies, beginnings or endings
Only the inner heart knows, by feeling, the flashes of lightning in the sky
The lost thought returns, on a sudden
Water pre-sets the rifts of departure in the mud
And, when the distance inclines towards the west, days will be left to the
side

The Yaoshan Mountain is where the crowd of birds has been gathering for

121

5000 years

The drumbeating at the altar has gone far away, separated by the three
layers of earthen colour
Even when the cloud and smoke have intentions, the flowing water leaves
no traces
A pair of widely opened eyes conveys the flight of the sacred beings
When the dawn of civilisation rises in the Meilizhou Sandbar, the banks are
boundless

(2018)

萨米兹达特一角

——悼孟浪

哈佛的午后。十月拐角处的门廊深邃
我俩聊起图书馆 samizdat 文库索引
仿佛就在眼前，竟成最后一面
美式咖啡的余香远未散尽
溯往事，八十年代上海滩
《海上》《大陆》《撒娇》掀起诗群大观前浪
《北回归线》《喂》《倾向》绵绵不息
你试图建起一座文献馆
笔下一滴血，滴成人类的太阳
映照校园满地斑斓的落叶
你手指海报 *In Other Wor(l)d* *
肢体表达意犹未尽的深意
那燕京学社的门廊
那一拜街的来来往往
曾是你海外写作的前哨
终于步出不见校门的深秋
那一刻教堂的钟声，一再抚慰你难言的悲愤

In Other Wor(l)d 蕴含《别处的世界》《换言之》双重的涵义。

(2018)

In a Corner of Samizdat

— In Memory of Meng Lang

Afternoon at Harvard. The corridor was profound, in a corner of October
We talked about the library index to Samizdat
Our last meeting now seems right in front of us
The aroma of the American-style coffee is still lingering
When I recall the old days, in Shanghai in the 1980s
There were magazines like *On the Sea*, *The Mainland* and *Sajiao* that
                        created pre-waves of the poetic spectacle
And there were also *Tropic of Cancer*, *Wei* and *Tendency* that were
                        continuous
You were trying to build a museum of literature
A drop of blood under your pen dripped into a human sun
Reflecting the brilliant fallen leaves covering the campus
You pointed at the poster, *In Other Wor(l)d* *
Expressing its profundity, not yet given full expression to, with your limbs
The porch of the Harvard-Yenching Institute
And the comings and goings on One Bow Street
Used to be your writing outpost
Finally, I stepped out of the deep autumn in which I couldn't see the
                        entrance to the university
And the sound of the bell, in that moment, kept comforting you for your
                        inexpressible Fury

*'*In Other Wor(l)d*' contains a double meaning of *A World Elsewhere* and *In Other Words*.

(2018)

一切都从大海出发

流动又静止，岬角处的湾流
流动一丝异乡的神秘
通畅又不失缠绵
远离大陆，大洋在两侧紧紧相拥

苍穹之下，不见一丝雾霾
三角梅灿烂的一瞥
潮水间红树林的倔强
虚化我十年来修剪的枝丫

落日与初阳，纯净又明亮
在阳台两侧位移
岁月的拐角处，流水依旧
此刻，晚霞高过现实的喧嚣

寂静，却蕴涵着无限的生机
起伏的内心与行星呼应
一样的脉动，一样的心灵
一切都从大海出发

（2018，《诗刊》·临高海上丝绸之路国际峰会）

Everything Begins from the Ocean

Moving or stilling, a gulf stream around the cape
Flowing with a thread of otherland mystery
Unobstructed and, nevertheless, lingering
Far from the mainland, the ocean gives it a tight embrace on either side

Under the firmament, not a shred of haze
A glance of the brilliant bougainvillea
The mangrove forest stubborn in the tides
Has rendered my ten years of pruning abstract

The setting and morning suns are pure and bright
Moving on either side of the balcony
At the corner of the years, flowing waters remain as before
At this very moment, the evening glow is higher than the commotion of the
realities

Quietness contains unlimited vitality
The heaving heart echoes the planet
The same pulsing and the same soul
Everything begins from the ocean

(2018, written at Maritime Silk Road International Summit in Lingao, held
by *Poetry Monthly*)

www.ingramcontent.com/pod-product-compliance
Lightning Source LLC
Chambersburg PA
CBHW030842090426
42737CB00009B/1079